Another Child's Christmas in Wales

Lynn H. Elliott

To John and Barbara
Diolch yn fawr!
Nadolig Llawen!
Lynn H Elliott

Drws Coch Publishing

ISBN 0-9654432-0-5

Published by Drws Coch Publishing,
P.O. Box 5373, Chico, Ca. 95927-5373

Dedication:

To Grandma Elliott and the begats and begats of Elliotts who made this story live--this gift

To Granddad and Grandma Humphries and the begats and begats of Humphries who made this story live--this gift

To my mother, Hilda (1913-1989); my father, Douglas (1912-1995); sister Yvonne; brother James; cousin Sylvia; and all the other actors in this story--this gift

To my children--Owain, Rhys, Gareth, Bronwen, Rhodri ,Veronica and Eric--this gift

To Yvonne's children--Mark, Matthew and Paul, their wives, Leslie and Marion, and their children, Martin Paul and Benjamin--this gift

To Dennis, Derek, Gloria and Josie--this gift

And especially to Jennie for her love, patience and encouragement--this gift.

Acknowledgments:

Yvonne, Dennis and Sylvia for their help in recalling those priceless moments;

Robert Burton, David Hargreaves, Mercedes and James Gilbert, William Ramsey, William Johnson and Cynthia Lammel, Dan Craik, Dave Abbott, Len Fulton, Clark Brandstatt, David Lloyd, and John Ward for their assistance, suggestions and belief in the project;

My wife Jennifer for her love, patience, delightful illustrations and editing.

Another Child's Christmas in Wales

"One Christmas was so much like another, in those years around the sea-town corner . . . that I can never remember whether it snowed for six days and six nights when I was twelve, or twelve days and twelve nights when I was six."

But here a voice says: "You can't do that, boyo. Dylan's already done 'A Child's Christmas in Wales'."

Hordes of forlorn Welsh children, feet dragging through snow and rain, cross the English border, refugees in the homes of kindly Anglo-Saxon families for the Christmas season.

"Wait!" I cry. "Dylan wasn't the only one. When I was a child, I spent my Christmases in Wales, too."

Abruptly the host of Welsh youngsters turns on its heels and squealing with joy crashes up and over Offa's dike to be welcomed back by its native Welsh hills, joyous parents and bleating sheep. Croeso i Gymru.

****

Time to bring out the cascades of twisted green-and-red ribbons dipping and rising from walls and ceilings, the Christmas trees teeming with stars, lights and ornaments, and the mobile plastic reindeers, one with the unmistakable incandescent red nose, which all mystically appeared, overnight, in James Howells' department store, Queen Street, heralding the beginning of Christmas season in the sea-faring capital city of Wales, Cardiff. I am four, five, six, seven, eight, nine, ten and eleven years old, chocked full with accumulated memories of food, joy, song, and jolly, wind-swept shoppers.

After the decorations came the jolly Father Christmas with his cigarette-and-mint Polo breath, positioning himself upon the red velvet throne in the center of the store, his cast-iron knees molded for wriggling children to sit upon and wish and dream. My mother and I followed those dipping green-and-red ribbons and the host of giggling green-and-red children to the back of the store, the abode of the strange and mysterious bazaar ride, where a decorated sea-faring cabin rose and fell with each engineered wave. We sat upon the wooden benches and, aided by the well-rehearsed speech of a pimply teenage boson, sailed far away to foreign lands painted upon rolls of newsprint, revolving reverentially past our sea-faring portholes.

"On your right," monotoned the voice of our pimply teenage boson, "the Loch Ness monster rears its ugly head seeking out boats to destroy and little children to devour. Oh dear, oh dear. I think it has spied our boat." Little girls gasped and clutched their mother's arms. Eleven-year-old boys like myself gulped in terror, knowing that if we were only twelve years old, we'd wrestle the monster, throw it on its back and tickle its stomach until it promised to leave and never return again.

Despite the boson's droning voice, never once did I refuse to believe. I had left James Howells' store, Cardiff, and was sailing across monster-spawning oceans to exotic palm treed islands.

The voice droned on. "On your left the natives in their grass skirts welcome us to their sun-filled island paradise dancing their traditional hula dance."

At the end of three carefully engineered minutes, we sailed into our home port. Our boson tendered dire predictions about what would happen to little boys who dared stand up before the last wave rocked beneath our feet. One boy always did stand, showing off, and fell down in a shower of giggles.

The boat stopped, we leapt to our sea-wobbling legs and dutifully exited the front gangplank. Our pimply boson slouched to the back gangplank, where the next horde of child mariners prepared to clamber aboard and be wafted away to exotic climes.

The green-and-red ribbons, trees and fairy lights in James Howells' department store, Queen Street, Cardiff, spawned the sudden appearance of the many other green-and-red ribbons, trees, and fairy lights in all the other shops in Cardiff. In no time, the city was festooned with magic.

****

Years earlier, before my sister Yvonne told me, I would sit down and compile written lists on scraps of paper which, after my mother and father had read them first, "to check the spelling," rose through the accumulated-soot-and-smoke chimney. And, because I'd printed the address neatly on the outside, mine joined with the thousands of other pieces of child-written scraps of paper floating dutifully northwards. "You think it's arrived yet, Mam?"

"It's only been five minutes, Lynn. Takes a bit longer to get to the North Pole, don't it"?"

"How long?"

"Half hour at least."

We dragged out the atlas, heavy as the world itself, and coordinated time and place. Scotland, the Hebrides, Greenland, Iceland and finally, exactly on the half hour, c/o Mr. and Mrs. Father Christmas, North Pole.

But then came that fateful year when my sister Yvonne whispered the truth in my ear. Then I understood that it was not the jolly, white-bearded and cherry-nosed Father Christmas who grasped at these child-flying notes, but rather the parkkeeper ("parkie") at Victoria Park at the end of my street, grumpily picking away with his spiked stick at the thousands of burnt, smoky scraps of childhood dreams settling at his feet.

Rydw i'n canu yn iach iti, Santa Claus. I sing farewell. Gone, never forgotten.

Now eleven, the North Pole having been demythologized into my own home, 47 Forrest Road, the red-and-green ribbons heralded the beginning of present-hunting season in my household. Each time my mother or father went out, I crept into their room, looking under the bed and through, up, and over the wardrobes, searching out presents. Why this need to discover the treasure before Christmas, I'll never know, but search I did, until the tell-tale noise of the return of my parents, or, even worse, of Yvonne, stopped my search. "He's been looking again, Mam," she'd report, while my face and hands would contort into misshapes warning her of intended future reprisals. That night, under cover of child-sleep, the presents were moved a thousand miles from prying eyes--next door to 49 Forrest Road, the home of Nin Jenkins, a kindly spinster.

****

Bring on the carol singers. Some, like the local church group from Saint Luke's on Cowbridge Road, would, even after payment, continue on with a carol or two, before dutifully moving off to the next house.

But my friends--Dougie, Pam and John-O--and I, were of a different mold. Upon payment, we instantly disappeared, determined to sing as fast as we could before as many houses as we could, before the time appointed to return home and count our well-gotten gains. We could get through the first verse of "Good King Wenceslas" in ten seconds flat.

> Good King Wenceslas looked out,
>
> On the feast of Steven.
>
> When the snow lay round about
>
> Deep and crisp and even.
>
> Brightly shone the moon that night,

Though the frost was cruel,
When the poor man came in sight,
Gathering winter fu-u-uel.

We started outside Nin Jenkins' house, a guaranteed threepence, one week before Christmas. Then it was on to Mr. and Mrs. Griffiths and Mr. and Mrs. Thomas and the other people we knew. Finally, we struck out into unknown territory, where goblin faces bubbled around every door. Each time, over and over, good King Wenceslas looked out, and the poor man gathered an armful of fuel in ten seconds flat.

If no light appeared in the house at the end of ten seconds, it meant one of two things.

"Perhaps they're not home," whispered Dougie, his ear flattened against the front door like an Indian scout.

"They're home all right," John-O interjected, pushing Dougie aside. His fingers inched open the mailbox cut into the front door, and he stared down the hallway. "We know you're in there, hiding. Get your money ready. We'll be back. I'll bring my big brother too. Huge he is. Muscles like iron. Knock your house down with one blow he will." And with that, we were down the path and on to the next house.

"You don't have a brother, John-O," Pam panted, as we hopped from foot to foot like Eskimo dancers outside the next door. We three boys snickered, mimicking Pam's naiveté.

"He don't know that, do he?" John-O blurted between giggles.

On we went, up Lionel Road, down Turner Road, up Nesta Road, down Kingsland Road.

Good King Wenceslas looked out,
On the feast of Steven.
When the snow lay round about,
Deep and crisp and even.

But even the best made plans of rapid-singing carolers screeched to a halt, when that dear little old lady asked the never-to-be asked question: "Do you know any more verses, plant?" My friends and I shook our heads.

"Didn't know that song had any more verses," replied Dougie. "Thought Good King Wenceslas wrote one verse and then retired to his home in the country."

We all concurred, mumbling the words "one verse," "retired" and "country."

We all knew that wasn't the truth. I, for one, knew all the verses, front, back and sideways, beginning to end. I could guarantee that at the Elliott family gathering that Christmas Day night, my Uncle Jim would, before the family matriarch, Grandma Elliott, drag me to the piano and force me to sing and act out the young page to his Good King Wenceslas, my boy soprano contrasting with his breathtakingly low bass:

Sire he lives a good league hence,
Underneath the mountain,
Right against the forest fence,
By St. Agnes fountain.

The old lady watched, her mouth stretched across her face like a grinning hammock, as my friends and I huddled together. I stared at her. I knew her type. "Maybe another carol," then another and another until we were all caroled out for the night. At the end, she'd drop a farthing or halfpenny into our hands, and we'd croak, "Diolch yn fawr a Nadolig Llawen."

But this old lady was shrewd. She knew her carol-singing market, all right, knew how to get the best return on her vocalizing investment. "I'll give you this sixpence," she whispered, dangling the baited coin before our eyes.

We huddled together, wondering.

"You know any others, Lynn?"

"How 'bout one verse of 'Silent Night'? That's worth at least sixpence."

"What if she wants two verses?" queried Dougie, who liked to be prepared.

We all thunk our thinkingest.

"We'll give her the first verse twice," I blurted out. "Chance are she won't know, see?"

And so we stumbled through 'Silent Night,' our eyes fixed on the dear little old lady's sixpence-bearing hand, as it waved back and forth, conducting us. As planned, we repeated verse one when the sixpence continued its oscillations.

"Now how about one last carol, children?"

We huffed and puffed. Three carols! That was beyond the eleven-year-old carol singers' code of ethics!

"Can't do it, sorry. Gotta be home in time for supper. My Mam'll tan my backside with a broom handle if I'm not," I chirped up, lying in my teeth. My comrades backed me up, telling of the other physical tortures we'd all endure if not back in five minutes.

Through it all, the little old lady smiled that non-committal little old lady smile.

"That sixpence is playing damned hard to get," growled Dougie. "We could be here for days."

"She'll never fork over that sixpence," grumbled John-O.

"Given her three minutes already, we have," said Pam, who had a watch. "Let's go."

But we were transfixed, held in place by the shining, waving sixpence. The standoff lasted another five seconds before we stumbled through one verse of "The Holly and the Ivy."

For a few seconds after we finished, she remained, eyes closed, sixpence waving back and forth, our eyes impaled upon it. She was, in the non-singing silence, still hearing our soprano voices slicing the cold night air. Finally, after a child's eternity, the sixpence stopped waving and the little old lady opened her eyes.

"Nadolig Llawen, plant," she smiled, dropping the very well-earned coin into my hand. Before she could close her door, we were down the path, through the gate

--"Don't forget to close the gate behind you"--and up the path of the next house.

Good King Wenceslas looked out,
On the feast of Steven.
When the snow lay round about,
Deep and crisp and even.

A penny at the next house, and on we went. It was between houses on Lionel Road that Dougie gave me the news.

"Cracking, it is." Pam and John-O nodded in agreement.

"What's cracking?" I asked.

"Your voice. Wobbling on the high notes. Must be your time."

"What are you talking about?"

"Hanging lower, they are," giggled John-O. "Soon you'll be singing bass and chasing women like Pam here." A solid punch to John-O's arm from an embarrassed Pam ended this conversation.

We ran on from house to house, me desperately straining to hit the high notes without wobbling--but something was changing all right.

Every so often, I stopped between houses and feverishly calculated. "If we do one house in three minutes, we can get through twenty in an hour, and, if at each house we get an average of about tuppence, that'll come to sixty pence, five shillings, in an hour, and, since it's another two and-a-half hours before my mam'll come looking for me. . ." So much for the best-made plans of mice and Welsh children.

In our haste, we'd already bolted up the pathway and sung our mandatory four lines before Dougie lurched backwards and looked around, taking his bearings. "Dammit. 34 Forrest Road, Mr. Morris's house. You were 'sposed to remind us to avoid this one like the plague, Pam."

Pam's protests were cut short, as a form as solid and as huge as Africa pounded down the hallway, making ornaments and little children jiggle, as the earth vibrated. Mr. Morris, pot-belly fighting to escape from between his grimy vest and drooping trousers, flung open the door, filling it completely, allowing no light inside out, nor no cold outside in. He glowered down at us.

"I 'spose you all think you're getting away with four lines for this penny, don't you? No chance. The wife and I want at least three carols for this penny, understand?"

"Three carols," came the slither of an echo from someone somewhere.

If it was the wife back there, we never saw her. Just an unseen voice, floating spookily from behind this sweat-smelling behemoth.

"And none of your rushing."

"Rushing."

"Or your singing only one verse."

"One verse."

All four of us leaned this way and that, trying to glimpse the diminutive apparition obscured by this human Moby Dick.

"Start singing. Loud and clear."

"Loud and clear." For two seconds, we children stared at one another, our eyes daring the other to bolt down the path and hide in the lanes.

"We're waiting."

"Waiting."

But the thought of this giant catching us and squeezing us into tiny clay models of horses or chickens rooted us to the spot. The monster and his phantom spouse won their three ill-gotten carols, and we our well-gotten penny.

And I remember one house, half-way down Kingsland Road. We'd given our obligatory four lines and John-O was preparing to shout insults through the mailbox before rushing back down the front garden path, when we heard a faint tap at the window. The curl of a walking stick drew back the curtain a fraction, and the face of an old lady fixed us in our tracks.

"The door's open. Come in," she cackled.

"Hell, I'm not going in," said Dougie. "She may be a witch. You never know, do you?"

"She could change us into black beetles just like that," said John-O, who didn't read much.

"Not black beetles," said Pam. "Toads. And a handsome prince would kiss you smack on the lips to break the spell. Like this." Her lips fastened themselves to her hand, making horrible sucking sounds.

"No prince is going to kiss me," puffed John-O, summoning up the full strength of his eleven-year-old masculinity.

I threw in my tuppence worth. "If she changes me into a toad, there'd be hell to play. My Mam and Dad would sue her for a thousand million billion pound and we'd buy a boat and live on a South Sea Island eating only coconuts."

Tales of what small children could and would do with a thousand million billion pounds bubbled forth, distracting us.

"Let's get out of here!" said Dougie.

We were about to race to the next house when the cracked voice spoke again. "My son will give you a shilling."

"Well, that makes a difference, don't it?" responded Dougie. "Witches don't give away shillings."

"That's true," nodded John-O.

"How do you know that?" I barked.

John-O's head dropped as he mumbled, "Dougie told me."

Pam and I glared our "he may believe you but we don't" glares at Dougie. He didn't back down an inch.

"Read it in a big book, I did. This big." He arms reached for both ends of Kingsland Road.

That was good enough for Pam and I. Convinced we would not be changed into black beetles or toads, we crept through the front door into the darkened hallway. This time, our "Good King Wenceslas" was slow and loud, protection against goblins and ghosts waiting to snatch at rapid carol-singing boys and girls.

"He's down the hallway," came the voice from the front room. Unconsciously, we held each other's hands, drawing tighter and tighter together, a carol-singing blob slithering slowly forward.

A single bulb dangling from the ceiling in the back room was our only light. We were drawn towards it, like four unwilling, carol-singing moths.

"Maybe he's like that woman in that movie. The one sitting in a wedding dress all covered in cobwebs because that man never married her," whispered Dougie. We peered into the dull light, the dancing shadows creating images of a cobwebbed man drooped over his whisky bottle. There was a man, and there was a bottle. But neither were covered in cobwebs.

"The old lady in the front room said you'd give us a two shillings and sixpence if we sang a Christmas carol, mister." Pam punched me in the arm. My lie had sealed our fate. "Ribbit, ribbit. Which way to the handsome, toad-kissing prince?"

The bottle arched up to the man's mouth, then slammed back to the table. We backed out slowly, a trembling "Silent night, holy night" wavering through the darkness. Then the figure moved, slowly sliding his hand into his pocket. A silver half-a-crown appeared on the ends of his fingers. We stopped, our voices growing in strength at the sight of money.

All is calm, all is bright.

Down the hallway, in the front room, the cracked voice of the old woman floated frailly, dropping into silence on the high notes.

Sleep in heavenly peace,

Sleep in heavenly peace.

As we sang the second and third verses--the first one three times--Pam nudged me. "Someone has to get the money. I vote you, Lynn."

"Why me?"

"You don't have so far to go to look like a toad," giggled Dougie.

Somehow, amidst the giggles and punches thrown back and forth, our soprano "Silent Night, Holy Night" continued. I edged forward. My Mam and Dad's decision to have me one month before Dougie's Mam and Dad decided to have him made me the oldest. I sidled up to the man and scrunched up my eyes, preparing for the worst. My thumb and index finger pinched around the coin. For a split second, the whiskey-drinking, whiskey-smelling man and I were joined by the shiny half-a-crown, his alcohol-swimming eyes searching mine for his own life lost.

Come with us, mister. Leave your darkened, cob-webbed room, your darkened, cob-webbed whisky bottle and your darkened, cob-webbed life. Come with us out into the crisp, carol-singing night air. We'll run from house to house, singing as loud as we can to the nodding moon.

His arm dropped onto the table, curling protectively around his whiskey bottle. One last look, before I scuttled back triumphantly, treasure in my hand, to my cowering comrades.

"I would've got it," said John-O. "I . . ." His excuse was lost as we raised our voices, "Silent night, holy night," edging backwards down the hallway, past the cackling, unseen old lady in the front room, out the front door, down the path and into the street.

Now safe, we each checked the half-a-crown. John-O tried to bend it with his teeth and hurt himself. Dougie dropped it on the pavement, listening intently to its tingle. Pam squinted at the front and back, and held it up to the light of the nearest lamppost. All agreed: the half-a-crown was genuine. We were delirious.

"Let's go 'round the corner and buy a box of Cadbury's chocolates for ourselves," said Dougie. We dashed to the greengrocer on Cowbridge Road, bought the biggest box of Cadbury's chocolate we could, and emptied the whole box before you could sing four lines of "Good King Wenceslas."

That night, none of us ate our dinner. We were scolded by parents and reminded about saving carol-singing money for Christmas presents. "What do you have to say for yourself, Lynn?" asked my Mam. I could have fixed my eyes upon hers and, from the depth of my chocolate-churning stomach, bellowed, "Oh Mam, I was this close to being changed into a black beetle or a toad." But I took the easier path. I hung my head and promised that I'd never, not ever in my whole life, scout's honor, cross my heart and hope to die, spend carol-singing money on myself again.

******

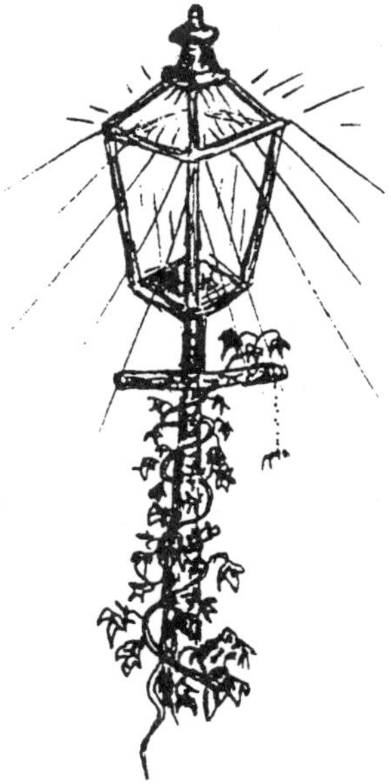

Despite all accumulated evidence from earlier years, on this, my eleventh Christmas Eve, I went to bed at six o'clock, hours before my regular bedtime, believing that I would sleep restfully until the appointed hour of seven o'clock on the morning of Christmas Day. An hour before this, I began my "O how tired I am" routine. This involved lots of stretching, sighing deeply, groaning, elbows sliding off the table, and my whole body slipping downwards in my chair.

"Tired, are you, Lynn?" my mother inquired, a smile twitching at the corner of her mouth.

"Maybe you're ready for an early night," my father joined in, with a wink to my mother.

I stared through forcibly half-open, half-closed eyelids, my head rolling, mouth open, out of mock exhaustion. "It's up the wooden hill for you, boyo," my mother said. And so I climbed the stairs to my bedroom, my father's final admonition ringing in my ears. "No waking before seven in the morning." My body said, "No chance of that," as it slowly fought its way up each ponderous stair, accompanied by a well-practiced groan of exhaustion. My brain, of course, was saying the opposite. "Think you're sleeping tonight, Lynn bach? Fat chance."

Our house had no central heating. What heat there was limited itself to a three-foot radius from the fireplace downstairs in the living room. We'd have to duck into this arch of heat for five minutes, and then spend fifteen minutes outside of it cooling down. Beyond the living room, blizzards raged. I crawled out of the living room, up the staircase and into the back bedroom, hopping and slapping my arms, as I tried desperately to keep warm. Before turning blue, I somehow managed to undress and put on my pajamas. Then I slid in between the two ice block sheets and wrapped myself around my hot-water bottle. Beneath the igloo sheets, I panted heavily, trying to heat up the air with my breath. Fifteen seconds into this, and the image of my parents finding me the next morning, asphyxiated in my carbon-dioxide-infested igloo, caused me to thrust my head out of the sheets and gulp in the sub-Arctic oxygen of my bedroom.

And so, to sleep on this my eleventh Christmas Eve, cherry-nosed from the cold, to wake the next morning, seven o'clock, fully rested, to the presents and sweets that lay at the bottom of my bed.

So much for that idea. I tossed and turned, until finally I slumbered.

But by nine o'clock, p.m., I was wide awake again. Ten hours to go! Ten hours! A lifetime! Nothing to do but accept time's fate and begin my calculations. Ten hours is ten times sixty . . . 600 minutes. Somehow that didn't seem as long as ten hours. And 600 minutes was only . . . 36,000 seconds.

And so I began, delighted that the calculations themselves had already taken about ten minutes--600 seconds, leaving me only 35,400 seconds to go. I could count to that in no time! One thousand one, two thousand two, three thousand three . . . Welsh sheep on Welsh hillsides, hearing the counting of someone lying in a horizontal position, stopped their grazing and began filing deferentially towards the nearest gate. Big gate, too, with all that wool on their bodies, but . . .

Heave ho--over goes the first. Heave ho--over goes the second. Then the third and so on until . . .

I woke at eleven p.m.--two hours later. Not my fault this time. Someone--transformed as the years passed from the corpulent red-robed cherry-nosed childhood myth into my father--someone was placing a large pillow case stuffed to bursting with its treasures at the foot of my bed. There it sat, taunting, eight long hours away.

I lay back, knowing that my sister Yvonne, awake in the next door bedroom, would, upon hearing the slightest sound, dutifully report me, as I would report her, if I disobeyed the seven o'clock injunction. Disobedience of the seven o'clock rule meant suspension of the squeals, laughter, ripping of bows, ties, and Christmas wrapping, and the stuffing of candy into an already stuffed mouth, until nine o'clock!

Time to recalculate. Even if I had a calculator, even if they were invented in those long ago days when Tyrannosaurus Rex and Anglo-Saxons roamed the Welsh hills, I wouldn't have used one. Saving time was not my object. The calculations in my head would subtract three minutes at least. One hour to midnight, then seven more. That's eight total. That's 480 minutes (nothing at all) and 480 minutes was . . .

At the end of Nesta road, the drunks wound their way home, their warm breath howling misty Christmas carols to the cold night.

Oh come all ye faithful,
Oh come all ye faithful,
Oh come all ye faithful,
Oh c-o-m-e.

A pause.

Come all ye faithful,
Come all ye faithful . . .

Grown men and women, who could, without a second thought, launch into Welsh songs--"Cwm Rhondda," "Sosban Fach," you name it--could not, for reasons unknown, ever learn more than a couple of the English words of Christmas carols.

Suddenly, reaching through the mists of forgetfulness, one of the drunken singers slipped in a remembered word, a "joyful" or a "triumphant," completely throwing his compatriots off. They huddled together, leaning against the red, round, dog-relieving post box at the end of Nesta Road, and discussed this verbal intrusion.

"Where was that 'joyful' then, Dai bach?"

"Duw, duw, man. You sure 'triumphant' was in this carol and not some other one?"

Finally, someone ended the discussion. "That's enough of that. Let's have a go at another one." There were a few false starts, as each sang his or her own private choice. And then general agreement. "Silent night," "Good King Wenceslas," "The Holly and the Ivy," beautiful carols which, even if the words and tunes were not exact, were sung with typical Welsh gusto.

By now my hot-water bottle had lost its primordial fight with the cold. I slipped it out from between the sheets to fend for itself in the frozen tundra surrounding my bed. In the darkness, my sworn enemies, the two luminous hands of the alarm clock, set by my parents to ring at the appointed hour, stared back, mocking me.

****

Whether I'd begun my calculations or not, I don't know. What I do know is that I woke to Yvonne shaking my shoulder.

Was I late? Had I, against all conceivable eleven-year-old logic, woken after the appointed hour? No! It was still night--but what a night!

Yvonne had scuttled over to the window. "Rose and Noel are at it again. Want to watch?" I leapt out of bed and huddled under the blanket with her, our noses pressed against the pane.

Rose and Noel, who lived across the road, were both a little *twp* in the head, and a lot drunk in the body. The drunkenness would fade overnight, leaving each with a bad headache; the *twp* was permanent. They were howling their versions of Christmas carols--little to do with Christmas, and nothing to do with caroling--to the unresponsive, dog-showered lamppost outside their home.

Rose and Noel lived in the parish house on Nesta Road, provided by the good deacons of Saint Luke's church, all of whom lived far away on the other side of Victoria Park, in the posh houses where decent people slept decently.

When Noel's father and mother were still alive, the Church had insisted that someone cut down the ivy slowly devouring the home. The mother and father, who inherited the *twp* from their son and daughter-in-law, refused, announcing to all who'd listen that the spider-and-rat-infested ivy was a Welsh national treasure, a work of art.

"Took bloody years to grow, it did. Those bloody idiots think they can bloody well throw us out, they got another bloody think coming, don't they?" the father would scream at all hours of the day or night to some non-existent being floating above him in the street.

If I saw any of the family lurking outside their home, I'd always take alternate routes, determined to avoid them. But, often, while slinking by, one of the family would emerge without warning.

"So what you looking at, boyo?"

"Nothing."

"House not bloody well good enough for you, is it? Don't think it looks bloody neat and tidy with all that bloody ivy over it, do you?"

The family member's high-pitched screeching at me soon brought out my mother. "You leave him alone or I'll have the police on you," she'd scream. I'd look for an opportunity to slide by and reach the protection of her arms.

"Bloody fools want to throw us out in the street because of the ivy, they do. Your stupid boy here bloody well agrees with them."

Here was my chance. "Who wants to throw you out in the street?" I'd inquire innocently, knowing the answer. The father, mother, Rose, or Noel, would point and screech upwards and outwards in the general direction of Saint Luke's church and heaven itself. Here was my chance to emulate all those Rugby heroes I'd seen at Cardiff Arms Park. I'd feign movement to one side, jink to the other, and then run like hell past the groping, screaming arms of my would-be captor.

And so the argument over the holly and the ivy and the parish house went back and forth, back and forth, until the good deacons of Saint Luke's Church, against all their Christian teachings, threatened to throw the whole lot--mother, father, Rose, Noel and baby Noel--in the street, if the ivy wasn't removed.

One night, when the family was sleeping, the father began ripping it down. He dragged it inside the house, up the stairs, and lay it over his still-sleeping wife. She lay there next morning when the police came, a latter-day, aged Ophelia, strewn with spider-and-rat-infested ivy. If she had floated like that, in her nightgown, down the River Taff, the image would have been complete, although unquestionably unromantic.

Beside the one affliction, *twp*, which left the family screaming at each other, the police, the church deacons, the King, Queen and Conservative Party at all times of the day and night, everyone was, as I remember, very short, in the four-and-a-half foot range. Rose, short and *twp* herself, had married into the family. Her head was, for reasons I never knew, completely bald. On top of it perched an Olive-Oyl wig, which slid from side to side as she jerked her head. Her mouth was bald, too, unless filled with the ill-fitting false teeth that chattered like a skeleton. Sometimes, as she screamed at me for nothing, or this or that, the wig dropped off her head and the teeth blasted out of her mouth. Both would plop at my feet, causing me to rush back home crying to my mother, who wondered as I secretly pulled at her hair and teeth, hoping neither would dislodge.

Back to Christmas Eve. Rose and Noel, drunk and *twp*, stood outside their house in their nightshirts, singing as loud as they could. Their parents had both departed to that neighbor-screeching, deacon-cursing, young boy-chasing, *twp* heaven many years ago, leaving Rose and Noel alone. No carols for this pair. Noel was singing "Cwm Rhondda" to the tune of "Men of Harlech," and Rose was singing "Men of Harlech" to the tune of "Cwm Rhondda" ("Bread of Heaven").

> Men of Harlech, Men of Harlech,
>
> Men of Ha, ha, ha, lech,
>
> Ha, ha, lech.

Yvonne and I stared out of the back window, our frozen noses stuck against the frozen window.

"Rose is on the job, you know."

"What job's that?" I queried. Yvonne giggled, her hand over her mouth, delighting in my discomfort about this secret, adult knowledge.

"On the job. Down the docks."

Visions of the skeletal Rose unloading cargo ships alongside hardened, sweaty, beer-swilling dock workers swam in my head.

"You don't know what I mean, do you?" she giggled.

"Of course," I replied, lost, but unwilling to admit it.

"That's why she disappears for a few weeks, and then the police bring her home."

I could figure out Rose's disappearing trick. Easy. She was press-ganged onto a ship and sailed to exotic lands like the ones in James Howells' bazaar. But I couldn't figure out why the police would accompany her home. Yvonne was staring at me with her "he doesn't know what I'm talking about" look. It was time to change tactics quickly.

"What if they look up here and see us?" I ventured. The thought terrified both of us, making us cling together under the blanket. There was no need to worry, though. Houses the length of Nesta Road lit up, as men and women, covered against the cold, screamed at the pair to shut up and get back indoors.

It was then that Yvonne pointed to the tiny sad, frozen figure standing alongside the screeching pair. It was Rose and Noel's son, little Noel, two years old and naked, shivering beside his parents, who had now added cursing the neighbors to their small repertoire of songs.

"Someone ought to do something about little Noel. Poor dab'll freeze to death." My breaths formed little clouds of indignation in the frozen air. Not only did little Noel have to suffer life in his father and mother's screeching, ivy-covered world, but here he was, freezing to death, while everyone ruminated, cogitated, and speculated, but did bugger all.

Little Noel's head waved back and forth down the shouting street. Then it stopped, fixed, staring up at me. As our eyes met, I realized, a trick of fate and it could have been me standing there. It could have been me alone, frozen, confused, as my *twp* parents wailed into the nipping Christmas air.

Suddenly, there was an explosion as Bobby Lloyd, a mountain of a man who lived directly opposite Rose and Noel, stormed across the street and grabbed up the frozen waif.

"Why God lets people like you have babies, I'll never know," cried Bobby Lloyd, as he hurled the diminutive Noel senior aside and embraced little Noel into the warmth of his body and his house. At this, the decibel level hit the heavens and beyond. Noel yelled at Bobby Lloyd's house, while Rose shrieked in her husband's ears.

"Call the bloody police, Noel. Hurl the bugger into jail, they will, and throw away the key." This, at least, was the gist of what she said! "Stolen my little boy, my only child, he has."

She prowled maternally--or, I should say, wobbled in her drunken state--back and forth in front of Bobby Lloyd's house, cursing him, the moon, and the church deacons safely snuggled up in their across-the-park beds.

Noel puffed himself up to his full four-and-a-half feet. "If you don't bring back my son, there'll be hell to play," he shrieked.

After thirty seconds, Bobby Lloyd reappeared. "It's Christmas Eve, for God's sake. Go to bed, the pair of you! Let the rest of us sleep!" But Noel, encouraged by Rose's screechings of the hell and damnation awaiting Bobby Lloyd, offered his own dire warnings of what would happen if he didn't get his child back. The mountain, sick and tired of these two diminutive tree-stumps, moved. Bobby Lloyd grabbed Noel senior by the seat of his baggy pants and his shirt collar, marched him, legs running at least one foot off the ground, and hurled Noel into his own house. Was the front door open or shut? I only remember a very loud crash and the tinkling of broken glass! A glance from Bobby Lloyd, and Rose ran, cackling and cursing, into her home, to attend her wounded warrior.

Bobby Lloyd marched back home, and Christmas Eve settled quietly upon Nesta and Forrest Road, Canton, Cardiff.

For ten minutes. Then the silence was shattered by Rose screaming at the police. The sight of this now bald, toothless, diminutive, *twp* woman, dressed in her see-through nightgown, was a real challenge to these two Cardiff policemen, who thought they'd seen everything. They tried not to laugh, but with Rose running back and forth across the street, shrieking as she reenacted the injustice, it was too much even for these stoic guardians of the law. Yvonne and I squealed with delight as the policemen, slipping and sliding on the icy pavement, lurched back towards Cowbridge Road, roaring with laughter, valiant knights of normalcy pursued by a cursing hag, who, in her indignation, frequently slipped, exposing all to police, neighbors, and the laughing moon.

Justice prevailed: the boy remained in Bobby Lloyd's house for the night, was taken away by the authorities on Christmas Day, and Bobby Lloyd was fined £40 for assaulting Noel.

Some weeks later, I saw a photo in a Sunday tabloid. A well-groomed, well-rehearsed, sad-faced couple sat holding hands, with the caption above their heads: "Give us back our baby!" It was them, Rose and Noel, complete with a harrowing tale of how the depraved and unholy authorities, for no apparent reasons, took their only child from them on Christmas Eve itself.

****

The Rose and Noel show finished, Yvonne crawled back to her bedroom, and I lurched towards the alarm clock. My eyes were closed, guessing, wanting it so desperately to be six o'clock. I squinted. Damn, it was only three o'clock. I wobbled back to my bed, slipping on the frigid cold-water-bottle, whispered an eleven-year-old's curse as my body slid between the glacial sheets, and began my recalculations.

I was awakened by a shattering ringing. This was it! Seven o'clock. The official hour. I kissed the face of the alarm clock. Yvonne, who always slept late, wouldn't open her presents until later, when everyone was gathered around the fire in the living room. Then she'd "Ooh" and "Ah" as she delicately--"Don't waste the Christmas wrapping"--opened her gifts. For me it was seven a. glorious m. Time to fill my mouth to bursting with candy, and rip and slash at paper and string, keeping me from the holiest of holies, presents earned by a boy who, for at least one or two days in the year, had desperately tried to be good. My room was soon a battlefield, the offending paper, boxes, string and sweet wrappings strewn everywhere. My hand groped down into the Christmas stocking, looking for that last little something. A walnut. What would a healthy, gift-and-sweet-seeking boy do with a walnut? This Father Christmas had a sense of humor--and a pile of walnuts to get rid of.

****

The morning of Christmas Day. Time to sit before the fire and try out all the presents. I refused breakfast. My apple-chocolate-boiled sweet-and-orange-filled stomach churned like a cement mixer. I was determined not to be sick, despite my parents' repeated dire predictions that I would--and soon. I lay on the carpet before the fire and drew on my magic easel. One pull, and my artist's renditioning of our cross-eyed cat, Tiddles, disappeared, to be replaced by stick figures of my mother and father. This was one of the simple presents, the ones I could figure out instantly. Another was the squeaking toy. I crept up behind the sleeping cat and blasted the high-pitched screech in its ear. Tiddles leapt in the air and scuttled off to find a better hiding place. Gradually, high-pitched screech by high-pitched screech, its hiding places were eliminated. The cat reluctantly scratched on the back door, willing to face wind, rain and snow, rather than this cat-annoying child.

Now came the unsimple presents. It sat there, neatly packaged, my Meccano set, an eleven-year-old boy's rite of passage into manhood. Young boys, future Frank Lloyd Wrights, with slim, delicate, fairy fingers able to join tiny nuts onto tiny bolts, sat before this construction set and created miniature marvels. But young boys like myself, unable to command my tiny nut-and-bolt kingdom because of my short, squat fingers, fumbled and groped, until we constructed--what? A bridge that looked like a tractor? A leaning skyscraper of Pisa, tottering precariously, waiting for its first--and last--earthquake?

"Maybe you could make something to take with you to the party tonight, to show Grandma Elliott," my mother offered. "She'd like that."

"What shall I make, Mam?" I queried. The world of construction was my oyster.

"I don't know. Maybe a skyscraper."

"Bigger than the Empire State Building," I offered.

"Bigger than even that," she replied.

And so I began building the biggest and bestest skyscraper in the whole wide world to be presented, ceremonially, to Grandma Elliott that evening.

But the Machiavellian, cross-eyed cat, Tiddles, returning now the squeaking toy was abandoned, had other plans for my Meccano masterpiece. The cat loitered high on the back of the sofa, awaiting its revenge. Blissfully unaware, I built upwards and upwards towards the heavens.

At the correct cat moment, Tiddles pounced, landing catfully near my newly constructed tour de force. The Tower of Babel crashed, destroying all its one-eighth-inch-size inhabitants. The Machiavellian feline scuttled off, chuckling catfully to itself, and I spent the next hour finding the tiny nuts and bolts lodged and cushioned in the thick rug, hidden by Meccano fairies who never wanted the little boy with short, squat fingers to touch these objects in the first place.

"If you don't find every last one of them," my mother warned, "they'll get clogged in the vacuum cleaner and we'll have to buy another, using your pocket money." All hail to thee, hallowed and holy family vacuum cleaner.

That Christmas, I also got a Hornby clockwork train. I set the rails in a circle, wound up the train with the big key on the side, and watched it pull its freight cars around and around. When I tired of this, I put objects on top of the freight cars: the walnut, pieces of the meccano, a shoe that wouldn't balance, and sent everything crashing over the bottomless canyon gorge. Then it was time to set objects on the track that unwary engineers would not see, so that the train would crash, killing all aboard. It began with paper, moving on to my finger, the cat's paw, my sister's finger, anything to cause a diversion and stop the train from just going around and around.

Last year, before the prospect of Lynn attaining manhood entered my parents' minds, I got a cowboy suit for Christmas. Dressed in my boots, spurs, leggings, chaps, shirt, gun belt, guns, waistcoat and one-gallon hat, I sidled out of the front door into Forrest Road, seeking a show-down with Billy-O the Kid, the bully who lived ten houses down from ours. Did Wyatt Earp ever fight in snow? No time to ponder the question, as an iceball--not even a snowball, but an iceball!--hammered into my ear and slid slowly, like a polar iceberg, down my once-warm neck. I reentered the sheriff's office, crying for my mother and vowing that next year I'd get a snow-scooping machine gun that would pepper the Forrest Road bully, sending him running for the cover of Leckwith Forest.

But now I was eleven, one year and a whole stage of life older. As I lay on the carpet pursuing tiny nut-and-bolt-carrying fairies, my mother sat in her favorite chair by the window. Here she watched the neighbors go by. "There's the Morris girl," she proclaimed.

What was I supposed to do with that piece of information?

"She's out early," she noted, giving me that knowing nod. "Too early, if you know what I mean."

I don't, Mam. I'm only eleven and I still have no idea what any of this means. But I said nothing, grunting as I continued my never-ending quest for nuts and bolts.

Suddenly, my father appeared, a glass of his prime elderberry wine, fermenting in large vats in the middle room, wobbling in his hand. "Try this, Lil!" he offered, knowing that my mother never drank. Without turning from her Morris-girl-spotting-window, my mother held up her hand, refusing my Dad's offer. And so he stood there in the middle of the living room, raised the glass to his mouth, and sniffed and sipped its contents. The verdict was delivered. It was perfect. No surprise there. Every year the elderberry wine was sniffed, sipped and declared perfect. And so, the Douglas Elliott seal of approval received, it was time for me to help Dad bottle and label the ambrosial brew for presents.

Into the middle room we went, me to hold the bottle, funnel and filter, Dad to fill the bottles. My father would take off the large sheets of cheese cloths covering the vats and stare into the mixture.

"Why are they called cheese cloth, Dad?" I asked.

"Because they're used to make cheese," he replied, dipping his index finger into the mixture and then, with connoisseurial expertise, sucking that same finger.

"But you use them to make elderberry wine. So why not call them elderberry wine cloths?" I inquired. He answered with one of those rational adult answers destined to confuse children since time immemorial. "Because they're not, that's why." And with that, we began bottling the elderberry wine.

The middle room was off limits during elderberry wine fermenting season. Once--I swear it wasn't me--someone left open the door. The cat got in, leapt on the cheese cloth, thinking it was a warm bed, and disappeared into the vat. The drunken cat was rescued; the vat of elderberry wine was not.

While Dad labeled the bottles and corked the wine, and my mother stared out of the window at the Morris girl, and I picked up the fairy nuts and bolts on this Christmas morning, my sister, Yvonne, carefully lined up her unopened sweets.

"Which one shall I open first?" she'd inquire to nobody in general, me in particular. "Do I feel like a Rowntree's fruit gum or some Cadbury's chocolate? Maybe it's time for a boiled sweet." She held up each item to the window, reading each ingredient it contained. The pressure was immense. I held on, determined not to satisfy her. I had to pretend I'd not even heard her.

"Fruit gums are so chewy, aren't they? I wonder what they're made of."

It was hell. Dear God, with so many choices at hand, why did You invent sisters?

****

It was ten o'clock on Christmas Day morning, time for our annual trek to the home of Uncle Tom and Auntie Phyllis. Uncle Tom was my father's brother. The rest of the Elliotts liked him but not his wife. And so, for reasons I was too young to comprehend--maybe her predilection for plastic penny-pinching, the pair was the black sheep of the family. This meant they were not invited to the traditional Christmas dinner and festivities at 284 Cowbridge Road that night, Christmas Day evening.

But my mother and father, kind souls that they were, liked my Uncle Tom, put up with my Auntie Phyllis, and felt sorry for the pair. And so, at ten o'clock on the dot, Yvonne, my father and mother and I would make our annual pilgrimage up Whitchurch way to the pen of the black sheep.

The whole visit was pure hell. Auntie Phyllis and Uncle Tom never had children. In the place of children, Auntie Phyllis installed thick plastic to cover the sofa, the chairs, dressers, whatever. Dust and little children were her mortal enemies.

We stood outside the door, my father with the bottle of elderberry wine in hand, and listened, as Uncle Tom shuffled up to the door. He welcomed us, gesturing at the same time to our feet. We dutifully took off our shoes before entering the holiest of holies, Auntie Phyllis's Taj Mahal.

Even at eleven and almost a man, my mother still maneuvered me, arms glued to my side so as not to touch anything, to the sofa, probably untouched since our visit last Christmas. This sofa had extra thick plastic for extra dirty little boys. I was plopped unceremoniously onto the plastic sofa, which screeched and squealed at this intrusion. In no time at all, perspiration gathered on my legs and every youthful squirm was greeted by a doubly loud screech to be followed by a "Shh" from my mother. And so my sister and I sat there, unmoving, breathing in the plastic air.

To add to my discomfort, Yvonne slyly, so Auntie Phyllis wouldn't notice, pulled out her unopened Rowntree's fruit gums and popped one in her mouth. My face contorted into horrible shapes, hoping I'd find the face, the one that would instantly turn her Rowntree's fruit gum into a tablespoon of ipecac.

Uncle Tom and Auntie Phyllis were an odd couple. Except for his teenage years when he worked in the coal mine near his home in Tonypandy, Uncle Tom had worked "on the dust" (garbage collector) all his life. He was a warm man with big Welsh open arms ready to wrap around his niece and nephew. (Somehow I knew the kid-shielding plastic was not his idea.)

"How arru, boyo?" he asked, refusing, like all people from the Rhondda Valley, to split "are" and "you" into two words.

My Auntie Phyllis, poor woman, was thin as a garden rake, and stone-deaf. She had a hearing aide which never worked. Every sentence, every question, had to be shouted as loud as possible.

"How arru, Phyllis?" my Dad asked.

She smiled, oblivious to the formal nicety. Suddenly, the room rumbled, and dishes and young children shook, as Uncle Tom, in his booming Tonypandy voice, repeated the question.

"Doug asked, 'How arru, Phyllis?'"

Whatever the questions, whatever the statement, she always said the same thing, “That’s nice.” Then the ritual was repeated.

“I brought you a bottle of my elderberry wine.”

Boom! “Doug says he brought us a bottle of his elderberry wine.”

“That’s nice.”

“Your house looks neat as a pin, Phyllis,” my mother chimed in.

Boom! “Hilda says your house looks neat as a pin.”

“That’s nice.”

Between each quota of speech, silence slithered, broken only by the squeaks and sucking sounds, as I tried, unsuccessfully, to disengage my leg from the rivulets of sweat running down the sofa. My mother gestured towards Yvonne and I, and nodded in the direction of Auntie Phyllis. Time for us to say something.

“Father Christmas brought me soaps and perfumes,” Yvonne declared, as I held my nose and put my finger down my throat, a comment on her presents.

I was about to ask why we said, “Father Christmas brought”--even after we knew, when the earth trembled.

Boom! "Yvonne says Father Christmas brought her soaps and perfumes."

"That's nice."

Father, mother, sister--that left me to complete the circle. All eyes focused upon me, waiting. My mind was feverish. I forgot every present I ever had in my whole life. I wanted to shout out, "Father Christmas brought me a bag of horse manure and dumped it on my sister's Rowntree's fruit gums and Cadbury's chocolate"--but the smiling eyes were now dissolving into a threatening glare. I prayed silently to the God of memory, begging him to help me and let me live to my twelfth birthday at least. And He responded. "Father Christmas brought me a cowboy suit and a Meccano set."

Boom! "Lynn said Father Christmas brought him a cowboy suit and a Meccano set."

"That's nice."

Yvonne chortled with delight. "You had your cowboy suit last year, fool!"

Boom! "Yvonne is telling Lynn he had his cowboy suit last year. Called him a fool, she did. Mixed up he is."

"That's nice."

The initiation over, Yvonne and I begged to be unleashed into the non-plastic back yard. A nod from Uncle Tom, and Yvonne and I grabbed our shoes and hurled ourselves through the kitchen, towards the back door. A deafening screech halted us.

"Don't let them open the back door, Tom. It'll spoil my cakes cooking in the oven." Auntie Phyllis, among her many obsessions, believed that cubic feet of frigid air were lurking outside, waiting to slither into her heat-tightened oven and destroy all within. My sister and I went out of the front door. Freed from the claustrophobic plastic living room, we threw snowballs at cats, until the neighbors yelled. We scuttled back through the front door.

Inside, Uncle Tom and my parents huddled together, talking. The words "284," "Grandma Elliott" and the names of various aunts and uncles informed Yvonne and I that this was adult talk, family talk about the evening celebration, the one to which Uncle Tom and Auntie Phyllis were not invited.

Through it all, Auntie Phyllis smiled, unspeaking and Sphinx-like. Unable to hear the adults, she fixed upon Yvonne and I. That unsmiling smile said it all: she knew things about little children that even little children didn't know about themselves! Maybe she was watching, hawk-like, to see if Yvonne was sucking a sweet, while surrounded by the not-to-be-touched-by-sticky-children's fingers furniture. When Auntie Phyllis looked away, Yvonne slid the Rowntrees fruit gum out of her mouth for a brief examination, before popping it back. "I think it'll take me another ten minutes to finish off this one." This was whispered to a brother one year her junior, able to stuff the whole packet of twelve fruit gums into his mouth, wrapping and all, and finish off everything in three minutes flat!

When Auntie Phyllis went to the bathroom, Yvonne, with that necessary flourish to draw my attention, pulled out her package of fruit gums. Without opening the packet, she counted how many were left. I wanted to break the silence and scream out, "Dammit, Yvonne. It don't take no genius to figure it out! There are twelve in the packet. You've eaten one. That leaves eleven." But I kept silent. By now the perspiration was an eighth-of-an-inch thick, and I was sliding slowly backwards on the sofa.

Yvonne took out fruit gum number two. The thing was only as big as a thumbnail, but the way she rolled it around in her mouth you'd think she had the world's biggest gob-stopper. I was in agony!

Then she took out another. Was she, against all past custom, going to pop two fruit gums into her mouth at the same time? No. Her hand slid slowly sideways, and she deposited the sweet on my knee. In a flash, I grabbed it and threw it in my mouth, a split second before Auntie Phyllis returned. Then my fingers crept across the thick plastic and squeezed my sister's hand. Diolch yn fawr.

We sat, brother and sister, conspiratorially enjoying the sweet taste circulating in our mouths. With Auntie Phyllis glaring at us again, we weren't allowed to chew. We just gulped down the sweet saliva and periodically shifted the unseen fruit gum with our tongue.

The huddled group--Mam, Dad, and Uncle Tom--suddenly drew even tighter. Time to discuss secretive adult information. As I sat riveted to the sofa, saliva building in my mouth, the word "dying" escaped from the clandestine adult group. The word slithered towards the couch, souring my once-sweetened mouth. I felt the urge to leap up and, against all my eleven-year-old rights, burst in upon the group and demand answers. What were they talking about? Who were they talking about?

Auntie Phyllis's stare fixed me to the sofa.

All was forgotten when, without warning, Auntie Phyllis hurled her own question at Yvonne and myself, striking us squarely between the eyes. "Would you like some tea and a biscuit?" Her query had nothing to do with tea or biscuits. It was a tactic to see if we could answer without revealing the hidden fruit gum, without spitting it out on the carpet at her feet.

Before either of us could answer Auntie Phyllis, an explosion--Boom! "Let's get something in that boy's stomach," my Uncle Tom proclaimed. Time to swallow the fruit gum hastily, to tremble at the thought of drinking and eating in Auntie Phyllis's hermetically sealed room. Maybe a foolproof and invincible strategy would save me from the purgatory and eventual damnation of tea and biscuits at Auntie Phyllis's.

When the strategy finally seeped into my throbbing brain, it was weak and ineffective. "Can I go outside and eat with the cat?" I whispered to my mother. The cat wouldn't welcome me, of course. He remembered the boy with the squeaky rubber toy from last year.

My mother giggled as she shook her head. I was doomed to staying put, or rather hydroplaning slowly backwards on the sofa. My mother, having swallowed her giggle, gave me that look that burned in stone the parental commandments: "You will sit still. You will spill nothing. You will drop no crumb upon the carpet. You will not break cup, saucer or plate. And, when finished, you will tell Uncle Tom, who will dutifully relay it to Auntie Phyllis, how much you enjoyed the tea and biscuits." There was no arguing any of these commandments. I sat there, a petrified tree in a plastic forest, as Yvonne whispered with her fruit gum smelling voice, "Better not drop anything!"

A plate was placed in my left hand and a cup and saucer in my right. This meant that when the large plate of biscuits appeared, I had no hands left to pick one off and put it on my tiny plate. My mother leapt across to do it for me. Still I sat there, cup and saucer in one hand, plate with biscuit in the other, trying to figure out why God had not given me an emergency hand to sneak out on such occasions from inside my shirt and pop the biscuit in my mouth. Again my mother came to the rescue, placing my cup and saucer on the plastic-covered table. This left me free to use one hand to pick up the biscuit. My mouth moved slowly towards it. I was tempted to shove the whole biscuit in my mouth, saving myself from the inevitable. But good manners and the watchful eye of my mother prevented that. One bite and I knew I was in trouble. Everyone watched as a crumb, as if in a slow-motion movie, feathered itself to the floor. Auntie Phyllis, who couldn't hear any of us shouting questions and sentences from two feet away, could hear a crumb drop on her carpet two miles away in rush-hour traffic. The offending morsel exploded at my feet. Before I could react, the vacuum cleaner was sucking away, threatening to drag me into the dark little bag, home of dust, spiders, crumbs and offending children.

Time to stand up and get my tea from the table. During my brief absence, Auntie Phyllis would, without anyone witnessing her, zip into the kitchen, find a rag and wipe off the perspiring sofa. I picked up the cup and saucer delicately. Adults held their breath as both wobbled precariously, as I transported them back to the sofa. By the time I dropped my anchor on the sweating sofa, half my tea was in the saucer. Nor was Yvonne giggling at my plight. She'd been told off for putting her sticky fingers on the plastic. We were both ready to leave.

Finally it was time to go. I rushed out of the door in my stocking-feet, landing in the snow. "Don't forget your shoes, Lynn," my mother cried out. Boom! "Hilda told Lynn not to forget his shoes, Phyllis!" I leapt back inside, grabbed my shoes and dragged them on. Forget my frozen, soaking-wet feet. I was free. As I stumbled through the snow up the driveway to our car, I heard the growl of the vacuum cleaner in the background.

****

Back home and a rushing into the house to stuff more stuffables into my mouth. But, in my absence, Tiddles the cat had wreaked havoc on the few remaining wobbly Meccano structures. As if part of the conspiracy against me, the rug had swallowed up the nuts of bolts of toppled buildings scattered during the feline earthquake. Time to spend valuable time seeking nuts and bolts once again, while the monolithic family vacuum cleaner glared down at me.

A glance out of her mother-sitting, neighbor-watching window, combined with some mumbled comments about the ever-suspect, ever-ambulatory

Morris girl, and coupled with that knowing-unknowing nod to everyone in the room, someway or other connected in my mother's mind, reminding her of the as-yet-uneaten Christmas pudding. After a quick reheating in the oven, the brown, rounded ball of cake was ready to eat. My spoon, a coal miner's drill, pounded and forged its way into my steaming portion. Mounds of pudding slag mounted all around me, as my spoon plummeted into the depths of the sweet-smelling, sticky "Christmas pud," determined as I was to reveal the carefully-placed coal-miner's pudding gift, an oven-baked coin of the realm. My mother's hand settled on mine, slowing my jack-hammer, plate-destroying, table-rattling, coin-searching madness. "You have to eat it, Lynn." And so, dutifully obedient, I heaped the steaming pudding in my mouth. I was on my feet in seconds, running around the room, flapping my hands, grabbing at invisible snowballs to hurl into my gaping mouth. The trick was to retain the thousand degree Fahrenheit pudding in my mouth, resisting the temptation to spit it out--in case. After a few seconds, the temperature of the pudding had dropped to a mere nine-hundred degrees Fahrenheit. It was time for my tongue to seek and find the roasting-hot coin, forged in Vulcan's Christmas-pudding-coin-roasting smithy. A few jiggles of my tongue separated the volcanic pudding from the blistering coin. I spat it into my palm. A half-a-crown! Diolch yn fawr, pudding!

Now it was time to watch my father embark upon the "I wonder what coin I have in my pudding" ritual. As I watched his antics, I imagined my Stone Age ancestors gathered around the fire, one hairy chef genius thinking to herself, "What if I was to place a dinosaur bone in the middle of the Christmas pudding--as a gift?" And then a second thought, "And what if, as a joke, the bone in father's pudding was a large dinosaur toenail that stuck in his mouth? Chwarae teg, wouldn't that keep us all laughing until next Christmas?" And so here we were, millions of years later, watching my father's primal antics. Instead of running around the room throwing invisible snowballs into his mouth to cool coin and pudding, he would rush out into the sub-Arctic backyard, hopping from foot to foot, as he sucked in the freezing air. Then it was back inside, pudding deheated to mouth-bearable temperature. What was this he had in his mouth, hidden like pirates' treasure in the midst of the pudding? No, it wasn't a dinosaur's toenail. Somehow, as his tongue moved deftly around in his mouth separating food from gift, it, that same tongue, also found time to speak. “I wonder what I have. I bet it’s a half-a-crown. Maybe even a crown.” Yvonne and I knew different--but we played along. “Maybe it's a rare coin, Dad, worth a thousand million billion pound,” I offered.

Finally, after a tongue-scorching eternity, the coin slipped through my father’s lips and into his hands. A penny, as always. The ghosts of my tribal ancestors joined in the annual guffawing at my father’s pretended disappointment. His act completed, my father was consoled with a drop of brandy poured over his remaining pudding--because it was Christmas.

****

Christmas Day afternoon--time to visit my mother's side of the family, the Humphries. Yvonne and I had filled the car with presents to be shown to uncles, aunts, and cousins without squeaky plastic covering furniture. Here was the time to compare gifts, to complain that Father Christmas liked my cousins Clive and Leslie more than me, because he brought them bikes with chattering bells. It was also time to pop Bassets' licorice allsorts, boiled sweets, Maltesers, Rolos, Cadbury's chocolate and anything else chewy, hard, and sweet into a young boy's mouth. Only one hindrance was placed upon my indulgence--that parental voice, claiming, "Lynn, you'll make yourself sick."

My Uncle Harry, with his broad-faced laugh, a blend of South Walesian joy of life and my Dad's elderberry wine, cried out to his wife, "Give the boy some more, Joyce! Give the boy some more!" And so it was with the many other Uncles and Aunties on my mother's side of the family.

It was also time to visit Granddad and Grandma Humphries. They were caretakers of Splott Road School, Splott, an unimaginative name created by some language-hating English bureaucrat. Here I dragged out my presents--yes, I set up the train track--no, I wasn't going to build anything with the Meccano-- and relived Christmas Day morning all over again. No plastic here, no fear of crumbs dropping like boulders onto the carpet.

Grandma Humphries ruled my Grandpa Humphries with a rod and voice of iron--except when he had a skinful of Dad's elderberry wine. With drunken bravado, for which he suffered until next Christmas, he detonated a yearful of repressed indignities. "And another thing, Elizabeth," he slurred, his finger waving blurrily at his wife, who sat waiting for tomorrow's throbbing morning to take her revenge, "And another thing. . ." After one too many "another things," Grandma Humphries stood up and gestured for me to lean closer.

Even in this my eleventh year, when I knew, Grandma Humphries pushed her fleshy face with its twinkling eyes towards me and said, “He’s done it again, you know.” I stared at my mother, hoping she’d help me out. I was almost a young man, ready to fight lions, set out on my walkabout, and listen to Grandpa Humphries pontificating from his once-a-year soap box. My mother gave me that “play along with it and you’ll get a reward” look. I gawked at Grandma Humphries.

“Stuck again, is he?” I queried nonchalantly.

“Let’s go take a look.” She jerked her head sideways, challenging me to enter the front room. I exited the living room and play-acted creeping fearfully down the hallway. Before entering the front room, I stopped and turned around.

“Sure, are you?”

Granddad and Grandma Humphries waited, staring at me. “We’re sure. Go take a look.” I swallowed back a malteser and slowly opened the door to the front room. Pretend, Lynn, pretend. I peeked around the door, my nose hanging from the door edge. There it was --as expected. Standing in the fireplace in the front room were a pair of long black boots. His boots. And tucked into those long black boots were red pants. His pants. And up the chimney, beyond where I could see, was the man himself, Father Christmas--stuck! Or so I thought, before I knew.

"Ahhh!" I ran screaming back to the living room and grabbed my mother's arm in mock terror. "He's stuck up the chimney and if someone doesn't get him out soon, he won't get back to the North Pole and his reindeer will die and I'll never get any more presents." Eleven years old, and still acting out this annual horseplay. Why not the giggling, applauding Yvonne? Why me? Would I still be doing this when I was fifty?

Returning home in the car, I got a grateful pat on my head and a Crunchie bar in my mouth. "That's for humoring them, Lynn." A Crunchie bar, my favorite--any time, Mam--even when I'm fifty. My father chuckled, "Catch hell he will, your father. When he sobers up tomorrow morning, she'll be waiting." The car lurched with our laughter, all the way back to Forrest Road.

****

Christmas Day late afternoon was time to return home and rest before the big event: Christmas Day Evening, the Elliott gathering at 284 Cowbridge

Road. Lying quietly in my bed, I giggled to myself. Despite all dire predictions, I had not vomited from my candy and biscuits orgy--yet. But my mother would leave a glass of Epsom Salts by my bed--in case.

No need for calculations this time. Rose and Noel, Meccano, plastic-covered sofa and entrapped Father Christmas--all rattled about for a moment and were lost in sleep.

****

I awoke to someone shaking my shoulder. In my half-asleep, half-awake fog, I tried to formulate my questions. Was Christmas Day over? Had I slept right through the night at 284 and into Boxing Day? No. It was Christmas Day night--time for the grand finale to this day of Welsh plenty.

Since the home at 284 Cowbridge Road wasn't far from ours, we'd slip and slide down Nesta Road and onto Cowbridge Road, the main artery to all points east and west in Cardiff. Yvonne, who held my hand, stopped occasionally to "Oh" and "Ah" at the festooned lights in the shops. "Hurry up, children. Can't be late," my mother sang out, clinging to my father's arm for warmth and stability. We plodded on, avoiding wobbly pedestrians and one-line-carol-singing drunks.

Oh come all ye faithful,
Oh come all ye faithful,
Oh come all ye faithful,
Oh come, come, come.

284 Cowbridge Road West was shared by two of my uncles, Jim and Arthur, two of my aunts, Margaret and Bess, and the Elliott matriarch, Grandma Elliott, mother or grandmother to all and sundry. It was a large house, with an upstairs and downstairs connected by a staircase with a banister for a young boy to run up and slide down until the insides of his legs were rubbed raw. The house even had an attic, the abode of unnamable, unmentionable phantoms, which this young boy never visited--in case.

Two dogs lived in the house, both unfriendly. Whenever the door bell rang, Major, a bull mastiff, was immediately hauled out to the back yard, where he could roam free, dreaming of devouring visitors to the house, especially young boys and girls thrown to him by Welsh Romans. A favorite game of Yvonne and I was to watch Major prowling in the back yard. Two gardens lay on each side of a narrow concrete path leading to the garage. Major would charge up and down this path, attacking enemies, real and imaginary.

The dare for us children was to wait until Major was at the top end of the path, about thirty yards from the back door, then open the door of the kitchen, jump out and make faces at him. "Nanny, nanny, nanny. You're a stupid dog." Then it was rushing back inside the house before this canine locomotive roaring down the path would devour us.

Once Yvonne, who now and then decided she never wanted a brother like me, dared me to do it. "He's only half-way down. I double dare you to go out there."

"I triple dare you," I replied, throwing back the bull-mastiff-mauled gauntlet.

"Rules are you can't triple dare until the person getting the double dare has done the double dare, then you can triple dare." I stood there, trying to figure out what this meant. She pronounced it with such one-year-older-than-you-are authority, that all I could do was stand open-mouthed, before figuring out that I had no option. Yvonne's thumb was down; I was to be hurled to the child-chomping Major.

I waited for the right moment and rushed out of the back door, jumping up and down and making faces designed to torment the squat, powerful hound of the Elliotts. "Nanny, nanny, nanny. You're a stupid dog." Major turned, saw me, and began the charge. I rushed to the kitchen door, grabbed the handle and prepared to dive back inside to safety. But Yvonne had locked the door! I looked from her, grinning at the prospects of being an only child, to the foaming mass of muscle and saliva hurling itself towards me.

Major was about to devour me, when Yvonne realized that life with me as her brother might be infinitesimally nicer than life-imprisonment, or hanging for throwing her brother to the dog. She leapt down from the chair and rushed to the kitchen door. But by then it was too late: Major was almost upon me. Nothing to do but grab the latch of the coal-house door and dive inside. I trembled in the lung-choking darkness, as Major pounded against the door, then sniffed and drooled, as he thought about chomping on my legs and arms. Even when he got bored and left, two years later, I remained in the darkness. When my parents finally dragged me out, I was covered in coal dust from head to toe. Here it was--a chance not be missed. Sobbing between each of my words, I described what happened, knowing that if I was good enough, Yvonne would be banned from the house and forced to go live with the gypsies on Leckwith Common.

"She locked me out! The dog wanted to eat me, Mam!" I panted and sobbed.

That night Yvonne went to bed with a scolding and without any supper. Not the full authority of parental justice I expected, but I was happy enough.

The other dog at 284 was an inside dog, a Welsh Corgi. Cariad was at first a playful ball of light-brown-and-white fun, pulling at little boys' socks until they fell over, or little boys' pants until they slid down. But then came the tragic day when some young child--not me--burst a balloon in Cariad's face. The dog went canine *twp* after this. It would hide under the sofa day and night, its moray-eel teeth and jaws emerging periodically to snap at and into the ankles of wary and unwary visitors.

****

Back to my eleven-year-old Christmas Day night. The Douglas Elliott clan gathered outside, staring at the festooned house bulging with the smell of the food, and the warmth of people, drink and song. All the uncles and aunts and cousins and nephews and nieces on my father's side (except Uncle Tom and Auntie Phyllis) plus all friends of the various members of the family congregated at 284 on Christmas Day night.

As we opened the gate, Yvonne and I dreamed of the gastronomical treasures on the downstairs table. It overflowed with its dripping bounty of edibles and suckables and crunch-between-your-teeth-ibles. The centerpiece was a monstrous turkey, sliced and picked at into skeletal remains by the time the night was over.

As we walked up the garden path, my mother gestured to the second floor window. There she was, Grandma Elliott, her face grinning as huge and as warm as a Rhondda Valley morning. She had pulled back the lace curtain and was waving to us. The unspoken words, "My favorite grandson, Lynn," wafted down through the whipping air. Not much choice, really. I was her only grandson. Male sperm count was low in this generation of Elliotts. All used up in the previous one.

My father held up one of the many bottles of elderberry wine pocketed throughout his person. A smile. Whatever the result, bitter or sweet, Grandma Elliott always appreciated her son Douglas's elderberry wine.

My mother gave me the once over, spitting on her fingers and removing a muddy stain that had mysteriously appeared on my cheek. Tie straight, cow lick flattened and we were ready. "Right, then!" my father proclaimed, glancing around the group. A deep breath from each of us, and then my father lifted his fist to rat-tat-tat on the door. Douglas Elliott, our poet Virgil, prepared to guide us into this warm Welsh divine comedy.

The front door opened and we were hustled inside to keep out the cold Cardiff air. The welcomings began, the prolog to the three-act drama on Christmas Day night at 284 Cowbridge Road. "Where's my Lynn? Where's my boyo?" my already tipsy Auntie Margaret cried out. I watched as this mountain of flesh rushed forward, swooping me up in her arms and hugging me into her leviathan bosoms. My little arms and legs flailed as I struggled for oxygen. Then it was the barrel-chested Uncle Jim's turn to welcome the guests, flattening my nose, face and ribs against his inflexible barrel chest. In no time, a whole host of wobbly aunts and cigar-smoking uncles swooped me off the ground and enveloped me in their monstrous warm welcomes. *Croeso, pawb.*

From above our heads, in the large upstairs front room, came the thumps, chortles, and fragments of piano music and song. This was the room where soon serious little boys and girls would perform seriously, before drunken and most unserious parents, aunts, and uncles.

"Upstairs to wish Grandma Elliott Merry Christmas, both of you," my Dad commanded. Yvonne and I raced each other up the staircase, crashing through the door of the front room.

Grandma Elliott, Sally, sat there, in the middle of the room, her eyes twinkling, as they revealed the begats of earlier generations and proudly surveyed the begats of this and future generations. Grandma Elliott's husband, Robert, my grandfather, had died years before I was born. He had entered hospital for routine surgery and never returned. And so it was Sally alone who sat here on this Christmas Day night. Yvonne and I plunged into her warmth.

"Smell my perfume, Grandma," Yvonne blurted out. Grandma Elliott leaned down and smelt Yvonne's hand.

"Beautiful. You'll have all the boys chasing you, you will."

"Have to be pretty hard up to want her, wouldn't they, Grandma?" I blurted out.

"I'm sure your sister has lots of boys wanting to take her out," she replied, stroking my sister's hand. "And what did you get for Christmas, Lynn?"

"A Meccano set," I chirped in.

"A Meccano. That means you're growing up," she smiled. "What did you make with it, Lynn-bach?"

"A huge tower. Big as the ceiling it was. And wide as the whole room. Mam and Dad been going out the back door and in the front door all day to get around it."

Grandma Elliott rocked back and forth. "A real Elliott, aren't you, Lynn?"

Mam and Dad, sister-in-law and son, soon joined us in this large collective hug for Grandma Elliott. It was then I noticed tears glistening in my parents' eyes. Why? The question came and went in an instant, as I chased after my sister, headed for the door and the downstairs delicacies. We dodged around Uncle Evan, already tipsy and trying unsuccessfully to juggle three balls. Yvonne's hand was on the upstairs door knob, when she suddenly stopped, grabbed my arm and stared at me. "She's dying, you know."

"Who?"

"Grandma Elliott."

"No she's not. We were just talking to her."

"I heard Dad say this might be the last Christmas she's with us."

I stared at Yvonne, then back at Grandma Elliott, wrapped around her son Douglas, my father, and Hilda, my mother. The word "dying" that had slithered so coldly onto the sofa at Uncle Tom's house earlier in the day was for Grandma Elliott. But she was there, sitting in her chair by the window, as she'd always been --as she always would be.

Don't go, Grandma Elliott. Don't leave us. There won't be Christmas without you.

"Race you downstairs for some juice," Yvonne yelled, already five steps ahead of me. The thought of Grandma Elliott's death had blown through the icy windows for an instant.

****

The prolog to the Elliott family Christmas Day night drama continued, as more and more people, known and unknown, poured into the already packed house. It was the time of introductions, of loud shouts of "How arru, bach? Nadolig Llawen pawb," and of arms and bodies locked in wild Welsh hugs.

Joined by my cousins--Sylvia, Pat, Gloria, Joan (as I said, I was the only boy in this Elliott generation's begat)--I ran up the stairs and slid down the banister at breakneck speed. First it was down to grab a handful of sweets and some fizzy "pop" to drink. Then it was up to the large front room, where the tipsy aunts and uncles were warming up to the evening by wobbling and croaking their way through some Christmas carols, while Yvonne played the piano.

There was always some invited guests, church-goers, who would know every verse of every Christmas carol, and would insist on singing the entire song to a thoroughly bored audience. "Did you know there are seven verses to 'Good King Wenceslas'? Gwyn and I know all seven." And while their voices wobbled through all the verses, uncles and aunts would ponder that universal question, "Duw, duw. Who the hell invited this pair, then?" Everyone, including the culprits, would deny knowing them.

Act I was almost ready to begin. But first it was downstairs again to the front room, deserted, except for the tall, fairy-lit Christmas tree, presents tumbling around its base, staring out into the gathering chill of the holy evening.

"Come see what we got you, Lynn-bach," Auntie Doll cried out. My arm almost left its socket as I was dragged before the tree. As my mother watched, I opened the present from Uncle Ivor and Auntie Doll, propelled into my waiting hands. My mother gave that silent nod that comes packaged with motherhood, that silent, knowing parental nod that says, "I don't care what you think of the present, Lynn. You will thank your uncle and aunt profusely." It was a pair of tartan socks--much too big for my eleven-year-old feet. "Thank you. Just what I wanted."

"Growing boy can never have enough socks," declared Auntie Doll. "I knew he'd like them, Ivor." My Uncle Ivor stared at me, an "I'm sorry, bach" stamped across his eyes. If only he'd chosen my present, I'd now have a potato gun in my hand. I'd run throughout the house thrusting the tiny cylinder into a potato, and firing the plug at unsuspecting cats, dogs, or drunken uncles. I pinched the socks clinically between my thumb and forefinger and transported them like some over-sized tartan bug to my mother's waiting hand.

Here, lying under the Christmas tree, were the practical presents--wallets, socks, coin purses--given a young nephew still learning the "whys and wherefores" of the world. I swallowed my disappointments and performed my necessary thank yous to perfection. The audience--mother, father, uncles, aunts--nodded approvingly. Now and again, from those uncles and aunts who forgot or didn't have time, a more acceptable coin of the realm was dropped deep into a pocket to buy sweets the next day.

Leaving my mother to stuff all the practical presents into a bag, I rushed off to the downstairs living room to fill my mouth, hands and pockets with sweets. My cousins and I took turns standing on a chair in the kitchen, looking through the window into the backyard. Here my Auntie Margaret, large bosom filled with goodwill to humanity, and large stomach filled with elderberry wine and whatever else it would hold, warbled her alto, hands held together professionally like an opera singer, to the patient moon. Alongside her, Major the bull mastiff howled his baritone howls.

Come into the garden, Maude
The blackbird, night, has flown.

She had, she thought, found a secluded spot, far from the maddening crowd, to rehearse her party piece, unsung since last year.

"She sang that same piece last year," cried Joan.

"And the year before that," said Gloria.

"Maybe she was born singing it," I chirped up. "Doctors and nurses in the hospital trying to gag her as they spanked her new born bottom." We all snickered.

Suddenly, Auntie Margaret stopped. Major, unperturbed, continued his baritone bellowings.

"Forgotten the words again, she has," giggled Gloria.

Later, unaccompanied by the child-chomping, howling Major, Auntie Margaret sang this party piece again. She came into the garden with Maude and, once again, forgot why she'd came. Determined not to read the sheet music, she'd forget the words--again. "Don't tell me," she'd cry out. "I'll remember them. Give me a minute."

A sudden move from one of the cousins, and we all raced back upstairs. The church-goers were stolidly marching through the sixth verse of 'Good King Wenceslas' when we burst into the room. Here was the diversion Uncle Evan needed. He leapt to his feet, gathered us around him, and pulled two spoons from his shirt pocket. We watched, fascinated, as the spoons rattled up one side of Uncle Evan's arms and legs and crackled down the other. Good King Wenceslas, poor soul, gave up in frustration and slouched off into the lonely snow.

Soon everyone was talking and drinking loud. In those years after the war, beer was in short supply. So, in its place, came a witches' brew of anything and everything liquid and alcoholic. One year, one of my uncles had--we didn't ask how--got ahold of some bottles of scrumpo, a raw, raw cider. Tales tell of barkeepers offering to buy the unsuspecting a second pint of this potent beverage if the first was consumed. The barkeeper never lost. My uncles mixed this scrumpo with stout, elderberry wine, and other potable unmentionables. The result was a lethal mixture designed to set uncles, aunts and the unsuspecting, ankle-nipping dog into an instant Mount Vesuvian eruption.

****

The clock struck the appointed hour of eight. The prolog finished and all late arrivals and early departures completed, it was time to raise the curtain for Act I of this family drama. Grandma Elliott, the celebrated mistress of ceremonies, sat smiling as, she contemplated the boisterous progression of Elliotts she had offered into this sacrificial world. Act I of her evening's entertainment was by and for the children, sober youngsters who'd practiced their party pieces for weeks.

After a piano piece by Yvonne, a failed conjuring trick by me, and a few more songs by other cousins, the serious competition began.

"It's time Josie sang again," Auntie Bess proclaimed, pushing her reluctant teenage daughter forward.

"We've already heard Josie twice, Bess," proclaimed my Auntie Sue. "Time to hear my Sylvia again." There they stood, face to face: my Auntie Bess, thin and tiny, with a voice like a town crier, and my Auntie Sue, a roly-poly bundle of laughter. Except now, she wasn't laughing. It was the showdown at the 284 Christmas corral.

"Arthur," yelled Auntie Bess to her uninterested husband. "How many times has our Josie sung?" My Uncle Arthur was, at that moment, involved in his favorite sport: fixing the six-verse-singing churchgoers in a corner with his steel-blue eyes and arguing politics and religion. Without turning to face his wife, he yelled the first number that came to his head. "Three." It was not the number Auntie Bess wanted. Too many. She backed away and retreated to the corner to lick her wounds, drink her witches' brew, and keep better count.

And so my cousin Sylvia was propelled to the piano by her proud mother, Auntie Sue. Sylvia, who later took lessons and considered an operatic career, launched into Puccini's "O Mio Babbino Caro" from *Gianni Schicchi.* She sang warmly and sincerely to her father, my Uncle Harry Evans, a man who rarely laughed, and who became more and more morose and torpid as he drank. Sylvia was a songbird, a contralto Orpheus, Orphea, desperately attempting to melt the unmeltable, to enchant the unenchantable. She was a smiling, loving thrush, whose notes splattered against this unemotional, immovable object.

O, my beloved father,
I love him, yes I do.
I'll go to Porta Rossa,
To buy his wedding ring.

"Harry," my Aunt Sue, Sylvia's mother, chimed in. "Your daughter's singing to you. Are you listening?" He remained asleep, silent, offering a snort at the most. Then, as Sylvia ended, kneeling dramatically before her father, he snored drunkenly.

These were the early hours of Christmas Day night, when we could, with the exception of Uncle Harry, expect our uncles and aunts to listen to us. The room was a whirlwind of full-throated musical recitals: "One Fine Day" from Puccini's *Madam Butterfly*, Handel's "Largo," "Dafydd Y Garreg Wen," floated harmonically from wall to wall. Throughout, my sister, an accomplished pianist, tripped her slim, tinkling fingers over the keyboard, moving easily between opera, folk songs, and Christmas carols. Each musical offering was punctuated by another failed conjuring trick, a tap dance, poetry recital, or story.

I was on my feet, arms raised, legs spread wide histrionically. "Into the valley of death rode the seven hundred," I intoned. My arms fell undramatically, as I stopped and looked around the room. "I've forgotten, Mam. Was it seven hundred or five hundred?" The adults giggled as my mother ran across and whispered the answer in my ear. Up went my arms once more, and on I stumbled, knowing that this was only a warm-up to the magnificent party piece I'd prepared for later.

My poem finished, I sat on the floor before Grandma Elliott. While Auntie Bess and Auntie Sue stood, once again, face-to-face in center stage, continuing their gunfight, I recited all the presents Father Christmas had brought me.

"You didn't get sick from all the candy, did you, Lynn?" chuckled Grandma Elliott, knowing the answer before I gave it.

"Got a stomach like iron," I joked.

She slipped her hand into her pocket, and, looking around to make sure no one was watching, unwrapped a boiled sweet and popped it into my ever-open mouth. I leaned my head against her knees and wrapped my arms around her frail legs.

Don't go, Grandma Elliott. Don't leave us. There won't be Christmas without you.

****

It was time for Act II, that transitory time when the serious and the unserious blended. Now diligent youngsters who'd practiced had to share the stage with semi-drunken adults who either hadn't practiced, or who had an annual party piece they thought they remembered from last year.

Uncle Jim stepped forward, his bald head shinier and his W.C. Fields nose larger and redder after so much drink. The room resonated with the deep bass of the first of his many party pieces.

Speak to me, speak to me, Flora,

Speak to me once again.

He'd only managed these two lines, when his wife, Auntie Margaret, shrieked out, "I wish Flora would bloody well speak to him. Then we wouldn't have to listen to him wailing out this damn song every year." The room rocked with laughter. Undaunted, Uncle Jim stumbled on through a few more lines before forgetting the piece entirely.

"Maybe Uncle Jim should practice more often," I whispered. My suggestion was met with a prolonged "Shh" from my mother, the only adult in the room who didn't drink. Between acts, Howell Evans and his wife, Pat, leapt to their feet to tell jokes. It was still early, Act II. The children were awake. The jokes were borderline tame.

After a few more errors and forgettings, it was time for something more weighty. My Mam, Dad, Yvonne, and myself stepped up to the piano, and harmonized the piece we'd practiced for months:

Hushaby my baby,
Slumber time is coming soon.
Rest your head upon my breast,
While mammy sings a time.

Boasting aside, we were brilliant. The room pulsated with applause. The Douglas Elliott family had pulled off another coup, something new and unexpected.

In the non-musical interludes, we played a children's game. This one involved the children leaving the room. As my uncles, still in control of one or two of their physical faculties, prepared to play the board game with all of the children, the Pied Piper, my Auntie Sue, led the innocents out of the room. Immediately, Howell Evans and his wife, Pat, leapt to their feet. Innocent children removed from Hamelin town, up Pontypridd way, it was time for them to slide quickly beneath the surface of decency to where the off-color, adult-only jokes floated.

Meantime, we children crowded in a giggling circle outside the room, as Auntie Sue explained the rules. "Listen up, everyone. You go in one-by-one." We all leapt up and down wanting to be chosen first. "And," she screamed above the tumult, "you'll be blindfolded." That quieted us down.

"Blindfolded? You mean like not seeing things in front of you?" I stammered.

"Not a hand in front of your face," said my cousin Joan, who was three years older. "Think, Lynn, you could fall down the stairs, crack your head on the banister, and we'd all have to chip in to buy a new banister."

As everyone guffawed at my expense, Auntie Sue held up the blindfold. "Right, now. Who's first?"

Nobody was jumping up and down now. Being first was one thing; being blindfolded was scary. Auntie Sue closed her eyes and let her hand descend upon the first victim. Me. I waited for them to throw me down the stairs, pick up the pieces, and toss them to the waiting Major in the backyard. But no. Instead I was led, blindfolded, into the front room. I heard the adults tittering and shouting words of discouragement.

"No. Don't cut that off. The boy needs that." Soon the other uncles joined in the fun, presenting dire predictions of what was about to happen to me.

"Don't put those up his nose. In hospital for a fortnight, he'll be." After a joking eternity, I was placed on a board and told to hang on to my uncles' hair for support.

"Not much to hang onto, boyo. Don't rip any out. It's all I have," chortled Uncle Jim, almost bald.

While the comments and jokes rippled through the room, the board, with me on it, rose steadily skywards. "Reach up, Lynn-bach. You can touch the ceiling," called out my Uncle Anfield. After a few more words of encouragement, I stretched up hesitatingly. Yes, there was the ceiling. I must be six-feet up. I grabbed my uncle's hair again as my knees wobbled uncontrollably.

"Damn me, my arm's hurting, Anfield. Don't think I can hang on," cried Uncle Jim.

"You've got to, Jim. We can't drop the boy. Break his neck, he will."

I clung even tighter to the wisps of hair, as the board wobbled beneath me. I was about to plummet from this great height to the floor below, to be loaded, blindfolded and flattened, into an ambulance.

"It's no good. I can't hang on," screamed Uncle Jim.

"Look out! The board's tipping," cried Uncle Anfield. "You'll have to jump, Lynn."

I begged them to hang on. I was too young to be flat. But the board was tipping and I couldn't hold on any longer. My shoes slipped and I tumbled out into the blackness, arms and legs prepared for the monstrous crash onto the floor six feet below. I'd only plummeted two inches when I hit the floor. As they grumbled about strained arms and too heavy a weight, my uncles had slowly lowered the board until it was just off the floor.

The crowd roared as I parachuted those two inches, my outstretched arms and legs crunching into the unforgiving floor. The blindfold was ripped off, and I saw the laughing faces of my uncles, kneeling, the board between them. Then it was the time of the roaring laughings, as everyone recalled my protestations and reenacted my actions when assuming my end was near. I crept into the arms of my mother. "Now it's your turn to watch, Lynn," she said, comforting me. I relaxed into her love and watched as the next blindfolded victim, a cousin, was led unsuspectingly into the room and onto the board.

And so the children came, blindfolded, half-afraid, one after the other. Gloria cried and wouldn't do it. As her parents comforted her, I noticed Grandma Elliott's chair was empty. She had left us, just like that, silently, without a word. "Grandma Elliott's gone, Mam," I cried.

"I expect she had to go to the bathroom," my mother replied, flattening my cowlick.

My cousin Pat was on her feet, marching up and down and twirling a baton. Periodically, the baton leapt from her fingers and caught some uncle in his unmentionables, which occasioned another spate of jokes, directed at the uncle and his wife. Each quip was accompanied by a "Shh, the children are still awake," from some giggling mother. Didn't matter, I didn't understand what they were saying. Some of my cousins laughed as if they did--which I doubt they did. Pat's baton was now twirling higher and higher, causing adults and youngsters to back away from the center of the room and flatten themselves against the walls. It had to happen, finally. Up, up it went and down, down, it came--nowhere near the baton-twirler's outstretched arm. Clunk! Another bump was added to Uncle Jim's already nobbily bald head. Despite protests from Pat, her parents, my Auntie Doll and Uncle Ivor, bustled her off the floor, lethal weapon held tightly in their hands.

In the brief lull that followed, the door quietly opened, and Grandma Elliott, looking unexpectedly frail and delicate, and supported on each side by a robust aunt, walked haltingly across the floor. The laughing and yelling dropped to subdued mumblings, as watching adults and children followed her fragile motion to the comfort of her waiting armchair.

With Grandma Elliott wrapped in the warmth of her blankets, it was time for more party pieces. Despite repeated protestations about his voice feeling raspy or his forgetting the words, uncles and aunts begged my father to sing "Santa Lucia."

"How come Dad doesn't want to sing, Mam? He's been practicing that song every night for months now," I chimed up. Everyone laughed, and my father graciously consented to sing. To this day, I still remember the words, in Italian, and recall his soft, lyric tenor voice rising gently to and hovering above on the high E.

Sul mare luccia
L'astro d'argento,
Placida e l'onda,
Prospero e il vento;

Venite all'agile
Barchetta mia!
Santa Lucia!
Santa Lucia!

Unlike past years, when he sang out the final words so forcefully, this time they stuck and wobbled in his throat as he gazed teary-eyed at his smiling mother. He returned to his seat to sober applause.

A push and a shove, and my cousin Joan was on her feet, ready to do her one and only conjuring trick, the one she did every year. Once again we watched as she turned her back to stuff the hidden handkerchief up her sleeve. Once again we all "oohed" and "aahed" as if completely bamboozled as she produced it. Joan, delighted, nestled in her mother's arms, a boiled sweet popped into her mouth. I smiled smugly, knowing that this year the Douglas Elliott family had cooked up a very special treat for Grandma Elliott.

But now Uncle Ivor was onstage, his long lean puppet legs and arms jiggling as he performed his party piece, a vaudeville number.

I saw Esau sitting on a seesaw,
Sitting on a seesaw, he.

Wasn't he an eyesore, sitting on a seesaw,
Sitting on a seesaw, he?

Back and forth, between the comic and the serious, the well-rehearsed and the well-forgotten, we wandered, in this the second Act of Christmas Day night.

It was at this time that I noticed Grandma Elliott's eyes were beginning to flutter. I shook my mother's arm and pointed to the almost-sleeping matriarch. Now for that something special, that something I would offer this year and never again. My mother quickly signaled to my father. Time for the as-yet-unheralded event known only to the immediate family of Douglas Elliott.

Under the pretense of going to the toilet, my mother shuffled me downstairs and dressed me in a suit with white shirt, a black bow tie, white gloves and a large top hat that dropped periodically over my eyes. Surprise was of the essence. To prevent wobbling family members desperately seeking the bathroom from seeing me, my mother covered me with a plastic tablecloth and led me back upstairs. I stood outside the door of the upstairs front room, little knees knocking like castanets, desperately practicing my words, praying I wouldn't forget them.

I heard the voice of my father inside the room. "Ladies and gentlemen--and you too Anfield." Laughter. "The Doug Elliott family has scoured the world, looking for a worthy act for this distinguished company." More drunken laughter.

My heart was pounding. Why this huge build-up? Why was he taking so long? Why was everyone laughing? Why was it getting so damned hot underneath this plastic tablecloth? The mounting pressure of these whys proved too much for this eleven-year-old. Flash! I hurtled down the stairs, tablecloth and top hat left behind, before my mother even realized I was gone. Her pleas, cajolements and promises of treats to come were of no use. I was scared, I wasn't going to sing, I wanted to go to the toilet.

Then, ever so subtly, she backed up that cement truck filled with adult guilt and dumped it all over me. "Lynn, this is not for me. Not for your father. It's for Grandma Elliott."

Trapped, I grabbed for the sweating tablecloth, launched it over my head and reached for my mother's hand. Locked inside my igloo inferno, my mother dragged me up the stairs. Once again I stood erect, stiff, not breathing, in the wings of the upstairs room stage. Somehow my father--maybe by singing “Santa Lucia” again and again--had kept the drunken crowd in place.

“Ready, Lynn?” my mother inquired.

“No,” I wanted to answer. “I’m scared stiff, I haven’t taken a breath in twenty minutes, and I’m going to pee my pants.” But instead a quivering, whispered “Yes” slipped out from underneath the tablecloth.

My mother peeked her head around the front door and gave the signal.

“Ladies and gentlemen,” announced my father, “you have been most patient.”

“You can say that again, Doug,” an uncle called out.

“Now I am proud to present, all the way from Hollywood, California, that star of ‘The Jazz Singer,’ Mr. Al Jolson.”

Without warning, my mother whipped off my protective sweat lodge and launched me into the room. Before I had sung one word, there was a riot! Here I stood, a comic little Lord Fauntelroy, strutting and shunting my body in imitation of a train, while the top hat slowly slipped down my sweating face.

Toot, toot, tootsie good-bye.

Toot, toot, tootsie don't cry.
The chu-chu train that takes me
Away from you . . .

Now I was circling the room, arms still gyrating, legs kicking out in front of me, a pint-sized human locomotive trapped in a cheering coliseum of palpitating spectators. Every few steps, I'd stop and throw the top hat dramatically from hand to hand. I only dropped it three or four times.

Wait for the mail, I'll never fail
If you don't get a letter
Then you know I'm in jail,
I'm saying, Toot, toot, tootsie good-bye.
Toot, toot, tootsie don't cry.

The song ended, the adults and children wiped the tears from their eyes before launching into another round of roaring laughter. I remained deadly serious, the only unlaughing human being in the entire galaxy. Then I marched across the room to Grandma Elliott, dropped down on one knee and extended my arms towards her. Without warning, the top hat dropped down, covering my whole face. I struggled free and began my second number.

I'm a'coming, hope I didn't make you wait.
I'm a'coming, hope I didn't make you late.
My little mammy, mammy.

Many adults, overcome by the mixture of drink and guffawings, lunged out of the room, seeking the nearest toilet to relieve themselves. I remained unmoved. My arms lurched this way and that, poking laughing cousins in the face, as I sang about the sun shining east and the sun shining west--without knowing which way was which.

I was told later that throughout my performance, Uncle Harry belly laughed, something--and who am I to doubt it?--very rare indeed. Some even said it was only the second time he'd laughed in his entire life, although I was never was told what occasioned the first outburst.

All I do know is that I, with child-like abandon, unsmiling professionalism and all the appropriate, well-rehearsed gestures, poured out my heart. I was up on my feet, legs and arms spread apart, top hat sliding down to my chin executing my grandiose and pretentious finale.

I'd walk a million miles for one of your smiles,
Mammy.

I stood there, the top hat hiding my head. I'd finished. Then, with an overly ostentatious flourish, I bowed to the family matriarch. The room pulsated with thunderous roars of approval and "encore." Then it was body-hugging, breath-squeezing congratulations from all. And Uncle Harry Evans was still laughing. So was Grandma Elliott, whom I hugged tight. "Don't go," I whispered, so even she wouldn't hear. "I promise I'll make you laugh just like that every Christmas."

A thundering rendition of "Jerusalem" by cousin Sylvia signaled the end of Act II.

****

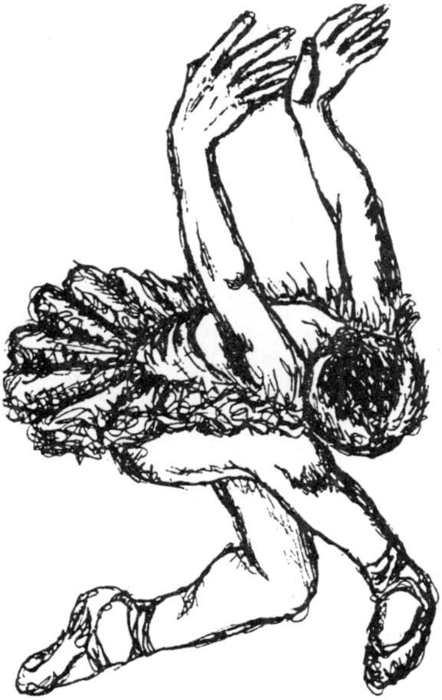

The clock struck ten. Time for the unserious, the giggling and guffawing, the falling downs and the forgettings of Act III. Uncle Harry, roused from his lethargy, joined, with wild abandon, in the singing of that operatic favorite, "I tought I taw a puddy tat." His wife, Auntie Sue, fluttered her eyelids as her falsetto squeaked the words of the anxious budgerigar.

I tought I taw a puddy tat,
A'tweeping up on me.
I did I taw a puddy tat,
As plain as he could be.

Then my Uncle Harry, paws crouched up to his chest, tiptoed around the room seeking out bird meat.

I am that great big puddytat,

Sylvester is my name.

The children squealed with delight, warning the timorous bird of the cat's approach. Each time Sylvester leapt, the fleshy budgie moved, making the cat miss--only to grab at a shrieking child instead. He licked the victim's face in preparation for his meal.

His feline imitation finished, my Uncle Harry, wafted along by thunderous applause and calls for an encore, retired to his chair to drink and sleep the evening away.

In a flash, Howell Evans and his wife Pat were back on their feet. As expected, their jokes in Act III submerged well below the scale of decency. Despite protests that the children were still around, the two precipitated themselves with complete abandon into scatological plenitude.

"Old monk in a monastery thinks to himself, 'Lived a sin-free life, I have, but never really had to confront temptation.' That night, down he goes to the village to the pub. Sitting at the bar was Geronwy Evans with his daughter, Blodwen, who had the biggest pair of . . ."

My world suddenly went silent, as my mother jammed her two index fingers into my innocent ears until it felt like they touched midway through my brain.

Trapped in this wordless universe, I watched as the men leaned back and roared their worldly-wide approval to the listening ceiling, while the women tittered behind their hands. As Howell Evans and his wife, Pat, staggered back to their seats, my mother unplugged her fingers. Yvonne, who had been sent out of the room on some fruitless mission, returned. The meal of the joke over, we could only watch the after-dinner reactions. Tears were wiped from eyes, before more roaring laughings sent yet another deluge down cheeks. Auntie Margaret, who belly-laughed as loud as any man, was screeching at the top of her lungs, "What a one you are, Howell Evans. Never know what you'll come out with next."

As we moved through Act III, the audience's level of appreciation was indirectly disproportionate to the liquid imbibed. So it was when my cousin Sylvia later sang Adele's laughing song from Strauss's *Die Fledermaus*.

The first part went well.

> My dear Marquis, you astonish me,
> I really must show my surprise.
> What can I achieve,
> Trying to deceive?

My cousin sang with teenage intensity. But when she came to the chorus--Most amusing, ha, ha, ha!--inebriated adults, led by Sylvia's own mother, Auntie Sue, joined in with their own rasping and strident "Ha, ha, ha's." Soon the "ha ha's" of the song mounted to an uncontrollable raucous laughter. My Auntie Sue whooped from the depths of her jostling fleshy belly, and then, all laughing air spent, loudly wheezed in all available oxygen before bellowing forth her roaring laughter once again. Sylvia had to be consoled.

Uncle Jim, whose trembling bass voice drooped even lower with each glass of witches' brew, now staggered to his feet, offering the assembly his last party piece. Beneath the thick eyebrows which lurched back and forth across his forehead, his eyes gleamed mischievously, as he slumped over unsuspecting youngsters and bellowed forth his song.

> Many brave hearts are asleep in the deep
>
> O beware, O beware!
>
> Loudly the bells ring, Sailor beware
>
> O beware, O beware!

Uncle Jim delighted in corralling youngsters like myself as he bellowed out his "O bewares." After one too many of these, I could hold back no longer. I burst into tears and haltingly confessed to my mother that I was not responsible for the death of these sailors. My Uncle Jim, delighted by my tears, unrelentingly pressed in upon me.

O beware, O beware!

I sunk deeper into my mother's arms. Uncle Jim, mission completed, returned to his seat and his drink.

"Young woman from England, traveling saleswoman." Howell Evans and his wife Pat were again on their feet. "So her car breaks down late at night outside this Welsh farmhouse. Begs the farmer for somewhere to sleep. 'There's the barn with my two sons,' he replies. 'No need to worry about them. Both *twp* in the head, see?'"

No need now for my mother to stick her fingers in my ears, protecting me from their even more off-colored jokes. The words swirled about the room awash with Welsh warmth. My eyes were fixed on Grandma Elliott. If I could only stay awake, she'd be with us next year, and the year after. But my fluttering eyelids betrayed my vigilance.

Between one fluttering and the next, Howell Evans and his wife had returned to their seats, and Auntie Bess had taken their place in the center of the room.

My Auntie Bess was, as I say, a diminutive woman with a voice like an air-raid siren. She sang in a choir, pronounced with her Rhondda valley accent, "coir," not "qoir." Having drunk far too much to sing, she decided it was time to perform what was supposed to be the "dying swan" from Tchaikovsky's *Swan Lake.* Between the flutterings of my eyelids, I watched entranced as the swan, glass of wine held trembling in one wing, a shred of lace floating freely from the other, pranced, stumbled and tripped, back and forth, back and forth, across the room. It was about five minutes into its "death" before even the most inebriated of my aunts and uncles realized that this swan was never going to expire.

As the swan rose and fell, rose and fell, a chorus of "Die, die, die!" and later "Die, die, dammit die!" began. The chant made no impression upon this cheerfully besotted swan. Blissfully unaware of the audience, my Auntie Bess's swan continued fluttering between life and death, until finally, after ten full minutes of life and death, the swan, wobbling from that lethal mixture of drink and twirling itself about, collapsed onto a sofa.

I forced my eyelids open, and stared through the laughing room at my Grandma Elliott. She like me was fighting sleep.

Don't go, Grandma Elliott. Don't leave us. There won't be Christmas without you.

****

Slowly the sights, sounds, and smells disappeared. I too was collapsing, not from drink, but from the tiredness of that long, long Christmas Day. I protested whenever my mother told me to rest my head. But I couldn't fight sleep any longer. My head settled into her warm, loving, maternal lap, the music and laughter gradually fading beneath my drooping eyelids, a curtain descending upon Act III.

I briefly woke up some hours later, as I was hoisted upwards to slump over my father's strong shoulder. Cries of "Good night, sleep tight, watch the fleas don't bite," "Nos da, bachgen," "Merry Christmas," "Nadolig Llawen," rang out, and wet kisses were smacked drunkenly on my sleeping cheeks.

I rumbled grumpily at the shock of the cold night air slipping up my pants legs and down my shirt collar. My mother tightened the extra blanket she'd brought along --in case. Yvonne whined. She was only one year older. Why couldn't she be carried?

Wrapped in my blanket and dangling over my father's shoulder, the muffled sounds of Canton, Cardiff, South Wales drifted in and out of my wakings and sleepings. I felt my father fumbling for his keys, open the door and carry me up the wooden hill to my bedroom. Only my boots were removed. This night and this night alone, I slept between the ice-cold slabs of the sheets fully clothed. My body shivered at the impact of the sudden cold. But inside the fire burned bright.

It still burns.